Building Grade 3
SPELLING
Skills Daily Practice

Spelling Strategies

Say a word correctly.

- Don't leave out or mispronounce sounds.
- Write the sounds in the correct order.

Think about what the word looks like.

- Think about how the spelling pattern looks.
- Write it, look at it, and decide if it looks correct.

Look for small words in spelling words.

- spin—**pin, in**
- cupcake—**cup, cake**

Look at syllables in spelling words.

- Spell the word one syllable at a time.
  remember—**re • mem • ber**

These strategies help me become a better speller!

Use rhyming words to help spell a word.

- If you can spell **book**, you can spell **look**.

Use rules for adding endings.

- Drop silent **e** before adding a suffix.
- Double the final consonant before adding a suffix.
- Change the final **y** to **i** and add **es**.

How to Study Your List

① Read and Spell

② Copy and Spell

③ Cover and Spell

④ Uncover and Check

Good for me!

Building Spelling Skills

Spelling List

This Week's Focus:
- Spell short and long **a** words
- Spell words with the endings **-ed** and **-ing**
- Add the endings **-ed** and **-ing** after dropping the silent **e**
- Recognize the short **e** sound in **said**

STEP 1 Read and Spell	STEP 2 Copy and Spell	STEP 3 Cover and Spell

fold

1. said

2. ask

3. stand

4. catch

5. eight

6. afraid

7. away

8. always

9. playing

10. waved

11. takes

12. than

13. great

14. they

15. prey

16. _____
  bonus word

17. _____
  bonus word

Visual Memory

Fill in the boxes.

stand	waved	great	than	prey
afraid	they	playing	ask	takes
away	said	eight	catch	always

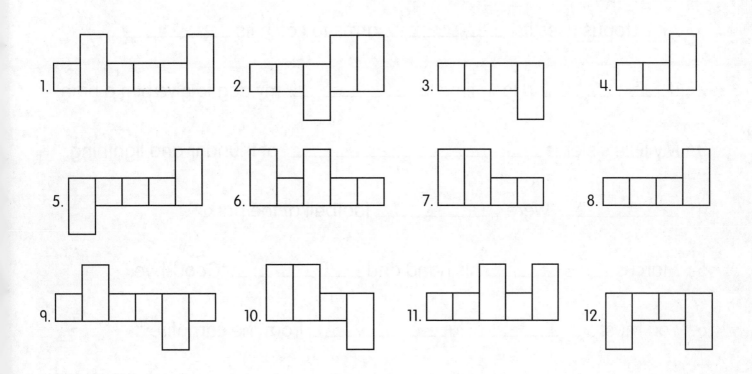

1. 2. 3. 4.

5. 6. 7. 8.

9. 10. 11. 12.

Cross out the misspelled words.

1. ~~sed~~   said   8. they   thay

2. eitgh   eight   9. aks   ask

3. great   grait   10. stend   stand

4. prey   drey   11. playing   paling

5. catsh   catch   12. taks   takes

6. afraid   ufraid   13. than   fhan

7. wavd   waved   14. away   uway

Word Meaning

Fill in the missing words.

takes	ask	always	catch	eight
afraid	away	stand	prey	waved
said	than	great	they	playing

1. An octopus uses its _____ arms to catch its _____.

2. It _____ a long time to _____ my dog to give him a bath.

3. My little sister is _____ _____ of thunder and lightning.

4. _____ were _____ football at the park.

5. Marcus _____ his hand and _____,"Good-bye."

6. You must _____ far _____ from the campfire.

My Spelling Dictation

Write the sentences. Circle the spelling words.

1. _____

_____

_____

2. _____

_____

_____

Word Study

Underline the words with the long **a** sound.
Circle the letters that make that sound.

w(a)ved   catch   away   takes   great

ask   eight   stand   said   they

always   afraid   prey   than   playing

An ending is a word part added at the end of a word.
Add **ed** and **ing** to each word.

	ed	ing
1. play	played	playing
2. ask		
3. prey		
4. paint		

Drop the **e** and add the endings **ed** and **ing**.

	ed	ing
1. wave	waved	waving
2. smile		
3. skate		
4. bake		

WEEK 2

Spelling List

This Week's Focus:
- Spell short **e** words
- Spell words with the long **e** sound spelled **ea**, **ie**, **ee**, **e**, and **y**
- Recognize the short **i** sound in **been**

STEP 1 Read and Spell	STEP 2 Copy and Spell	STEP 3 Cover and Spell

fold

1. next

2. left

3. help

4. please

5. believe

6. many

7. very

8. been

9. seen

10. she

11. between

12. three

13. easy

14. sea

15. leave

16. _____
   bonus word

17. _____
   bonus word

Visual Memory

Fill in the boxes.

very	believe	next	easy	leave
been	please	help	between	she
seen	many	left	three	sea

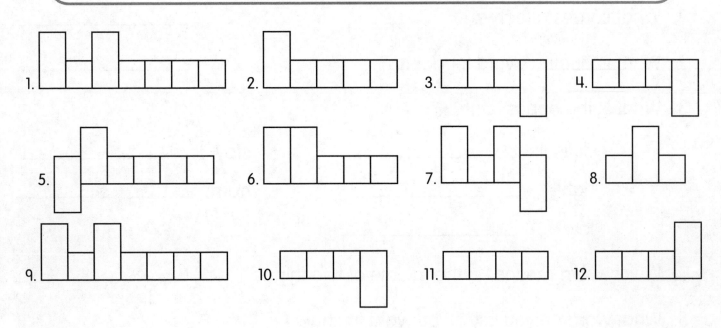

1.
2.
3.
4.
5.
6.
7.
8.
9.
10.
11.
12.

Circle the misspelled words. Write them correctly on the lines.

1. Plez help me fix my bike. _____

2. We have to leaf now. _____

3. It isn't eezy to ride a horse. _____

4. Have you ben to the park? _____

5. Park the car betwene the trees. _____

6. Did you belive his story? _____

7. I saw miny cows at his farm. _____

8. Jane had tree pet cats. _____

       Building Spelling Skills, Daily Practice • EMC 6593

Word Meaning

Answer the questions.

next	left	help	please	believe
many	very	been	seen	she
between	three	easy	sea	leave

1. What comes after **two**? _____

2. What is another word for **ocean**? _____

3. What is the opposite of... ?

   difficult _____   stay _____

   right _____   harm _____

   few _____

4. Which word means "in the middle of two things"? _____

5. What word do you use if you want to show good manners? _____

6. Which word means you think something is true? _____

My Spelling Dictation

Write the sentences. Circle the spelling words.

1. _____

   _____

   _____

2. _____

   _____

   _____

Word Study

Underline the words with the long **e** sound.
Circle the letters that make that sound.

th<u>ree</u>   left   she

please   believe   many

very   been   seen

help   between   leave

easy   sea   next

Write the spelling words that rhyme with these words.

1. merry   _____   6. pea   _____

2. any   _____   7. queen   _____

3. sneeze   _____   8. relieve   _____

4. free   _____   9. bee   _____

5. yelp   _____   10. lean   _____

next	left	help	please	believe
many	very	been	seen	she
leave	three	easy	sea	between

       Building Spelling Skills, Daily Practice • EMC 6593

Spelling List

This Week's Focus:
- Spell short and long **i** words
- Spell words in the **-ind**, **-ile**, **-ight**, and **-ink** word families

STEP 1 Read and Spell

STEP 2 Copy and Spell

STEP 3 Cover and Spell

fold

1. pitch
2. drink
3. swim
4. life
5. while
6. I
7. my
8. light
9. buy
10. eye
11. which
12. find
13. why
14. kind
15. try
16. _____ bonus word
17. _____ bonus word

Visual Memory

Fill in the boxes.

life	pitch	my	eye	why
drink	while	light	which	kind
try	I	buy	find	swim

1.

2.

3.

4.

5.

6.

7.

8.

9.

10.

11.

12.

Circle the misspelled words.
Write them correctly on the lines.

1. Mom needs to bie a lite for the lamp. _____ _____

2. Witch kind of drenk do you like best? _____ _____

3. Trie to catch the ball when I picth it. _____ _____

4. I get water in my aye when I swem. _____ _____

5. Eye like to by that kind of pen. _____ _____

Building Spelling Skills, Daily Practice • EMC 6593

Word Meaning

Fill in the missing words.

1. _____ have something in my _____.
   (I, try)   (why, eye)

2. _____ did you _____ that kind of soft _____?
   (Why, Try)   (buy, which)   (drink, pitch)

3. _____ kind of _____ do you need?
   (Which, Witch)   (while, light)

4. Can you catch _____ I _____ the baseball?
                  (while, light)   (why, pitch)

5. The words _____ and _____ rhyme.
              (my, find)   (try, while)

6. I have tried to be a _____ person all of my _____.
                        (find, kind)   (while, life)

My Spelling Dictation

Write the sentences. Circle the spelling words.

1. _____

   _____

   _____

2. _____

   _____

   _____

14

Word Study

Underline the words with the long **i** sound.
Circle the letters that make that sound.

l<u>i</u>fe	drink	try
pitch	while	I
my	light	buy
eye	which	find
why	kind	swim

Add letters to make new words.
Then read all the words in each word family.

ind	ile	ight	ink

_____f ind   _____ile   _____ight   _____ink

_____ind   _____ile   _____ight   _____ink

_____ind   _____ile   _____ight   _____ink

_____ind   _____ile   _____ight   _____ink

Spelling List

This Week's Focus:
- Spell words with the long o sound
- Distinguish between one- and two-syllable words

STEP 1 Read and Spell

STEP 2 Copy and Spell

STEP 3 Cover and Spell

fold

1. rocket
2. pocket
3. hold
4. told
5. often
6. grow
7. throne
8. so
9. sew
10. most
11. almost
12. both
13. coach
14. open
15. also
16. _____
   bonus word
17. _____
   bonus word

Visual Memory

Fill in the boxes.

rocket	hold	often	grow	so
pocket	told	also	sew	most
throne	almost	both	coach	open

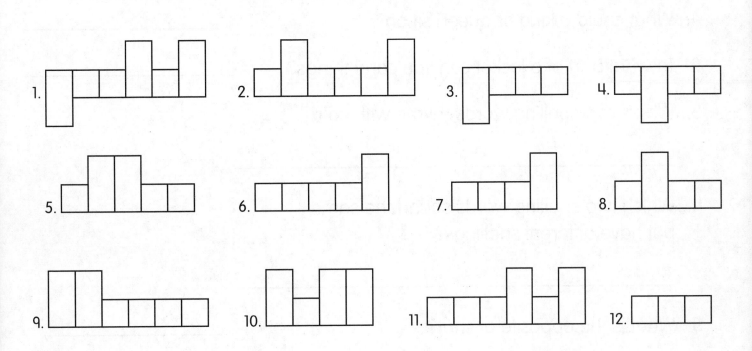

1. 2. 3. 4.

5. 6. 7. 8.

9. 10. 11. 12.

Cross out the misspelled words.

1. roket	rocket	7. coach	koach
2. whold	hold	8. allso	also
3. often	offen	9. opun	open
4. throne	thone	10. grow	groe
5. amolst	almost	11. told	tole
6. both	bofh	12. sowe	sew

Word Meaning

Answer the questions.

rocket	hold	often	grow	so
pocket	most	also	sew	told
throne	almost	both	coach	open

1. What could a king or queen sit on? _____

2. In what part of a jacket can you carry things? _____

3. Which two spelling words rhyme with **cold**?

   _____   _____

4. Which two spelling words sound the same
   but have different spellings?

   _____   _____

5. What is the opposite of **shut**? _____

6. What transportation would an astronaut use? _____

My Spelling Dictation

Write the sentences. Circle the spelling words.

1. _____

   _____

   _____

2. _____

   _____

   _____

Word Study

Underline the words with the long **o** sound.
Circle the letters that make that sound.

gr(o)w	hold	throne
rocket	so	pocket
told	also	sew
most	often	almost
both	coach	open

Say each word.

rocket	hold	often	both	almost
grow	so	pocket	coach	throne
told	also	sew	open	most

Write the words with one syllable.

1. _____
2. _____
3. _____
4. _____
5. _____
6. _____
7. _____
8. _____
9. _____

Write the words with two syllables.

1. _____
2. _____
3. _____
4. _____
5. _____
6. _____

Spelling List

This Week's Focus:
- Spell words with the short and long **u** sounds
- Spell words with an initial /**y**/ sound

STEP 1 Read and Spell

STEP 2 Copy and Spell

STEP 3 Cover and Spell

fold

1. under

2. such

3. much

4. young

5. touch

6. use

7. your

8. you

9. unit

10. cute

11. few

12. new

13. fuel

14. human

15. music

16. _____
   bonus word

17. _____
   bonus word

Visual Memory

Unscramble the letters to make spelling words.

under	such	much	young	touch
use	your	you	unit	fuel
few	new	cute	human	music

1. chum   _____

2. outch   _____

3. sue   _____

4. uoy   _____

5. intu   _____

6. wef   _____

7. lufe   _____

8. redun   _____

9. chus   _____

10. hunam   _____

11. sicmu   _____

12. gnuoy   _____

Circle the misspelled words. Write them correctly on the lines.

1. Jim's dog ran undar the bed.   _____

2. Do you like her noo coat?   _____

3. What is yer name?   _____

4. That's a kute baby.   _____

5. Don't tuch the hot stove!   _____

6. Ann's sister is a yung lady.   _____

7. A fuo boys came to the party.   _____

8. Do you like rap moosic?   _____

Word Meaning

Draw a picture to show what each sentence means.

Kate found her kitten hiding under the bed.	Dad pumped fuel into the tank of his new car.
The young boy played music.	A few pennies were in the cute piggy bank.

My Spelling Dictation

Write the sentences. Circle the spelling words.

1. _____

_____

_____

2. _____

_____

_____

22

Word Study

Underline the words with the long **u** sound.
Circle the letters that make that sound.

u̲se	such	few
young	music	under
your	you	unit
cute	much	new
fuel	human	touch

Write the spelling words that rhyme with these words.

1. crutch   _____

2. sung   _____

3. thunder   _____

4. shoes   _____

5. too   _____

6. flute   _____

7. few   _____

8. jewel   _____

9. Dutch   _____

10. tour   _____

Fill in the blanks with rhyming word pairs from above.

1. Zeke hid _____ the bed when he heard _____.

2. They bought a _____ pairs of _____ shoes.

3. A _____ little girl played music on her _____.

Spelling List

This Week's Focus:
- Spell words that end with a silent **e**
- Spell homophones
- Compare past and present tense verbs

STEP 1 Read and Spell

STEP 2 Copy and Spell

STEP 3 Cover and Spell

fold

1. save
2. give
3. have
4. live
5. move
6. above
7. alive
8. alike
9. to
10. two
11. too
12. know
13. do
14. blew
15. blue
16. _____
    bonus word
17. _____
    bonus word

Visual Memory

Fill in the missing letters.

save	give	have	live	move
above	alike	alive	to	two
too	know	do	blew	blue

_____oo   _____ike   _____ew   _____ow

_____ue   _____wo   _____o   _____o

_____ove   _____ove   _____ave   _____ave

_____ive   _____ive   _____ive

Circle the misspelled words.
Write them correctly on the lines.

1. There were tow plants in the pot.   _____

2. The girls looked ulike.   _____

3. His new bike is blew.   _____

4. Do you no what fish like to eat?   _____

5. May I hav a ride to school?   _____

6. Will you geve me some milk?   _____

7. Nat went too the zoo.   _____

8. Moov your bike out of the street.   _____

Word Meaning

Homophones are words that sound alike but have different spellings and meanings.

Choose the correct homophone for each sentence.

1. That little boy is _____ years old.
   (to, two, too)

2. I want an ice-cream cone, _____.
   (to, two, too)

3. Bring the plates _____ the table.
   (to, two, too)

4. A strong wind _____ the leaves off the trees.
   (blew, blue)

5. Did you see how _____ the sky was today?
   (blew, blue)

6. When will you _____ if you can go on the trip?
   (know, no)

7. There is _____ more peanut butter in the jar.
   (know, no)

My Spelling Dictation

Write the sentences. Circle the spelling words.

1. _____

   _____

   _____

2. _____

   _____

   _____

Word Study

A present tense verb tells about what is happening **NOW**.
A past tense verb tells about what happened before.
Use the spelling list to find the present tense for each past tense verb.
Write the present tense words on the lines.

past tense	present tense	past tense	present tense
1. gave	_____	5. blew	_____
2. moved	_____	6. did	_____
3. lived	_____	7. had	_____
4. knew	_____	8. saved	_____

Fill in the correct verb form.

1. New people just _____ in next door.
   (move)

2. Do you _____ how to make toast?
   (know)

3. The man _____ up balloons and made animals out of them.
   (blow)

4. Have you _____ the money you need for a new bike?
   (save)

Draw lines to match these words to their opposites.

alive	different
alike	below
above	dead

WEEK 7

Spelling List

This Week's Focus:
• Spell words with double consonants
• Divide words into syllables

STEP 1 Read and Spell	STEP 2 Copy and Spell	STEP 3 Cover and Spell

fold

1. missed

2. willing

3. balloon

4. spelling

5. pretty

6. still

7. off

8. added

9. letter

10. different

11. pattern

12. middle

13. Mississippi

14. zipper

15. carry

16. _____
    bonus word

17. _____
    bonus word

Visual Memory

Find the words hiding in this puzzle.

```
m b a l l o o n o f f x l
i i l l z i p m i d d l e
s o s w i l l i n g i z t
s c a s s y z g o o f a t
e t s t i l l i u v f d e
d g i p a s l i p p e d r
c o l r o w s n o p r e p
a z l e t t r i n e e d r
r p a t t e r n p l n r e
r o p t d i f f u p t z t
y f e y o s p e l l i n g
```

added
balloon
carry
different
letter
middle
missed
Mississippi
off
pattern
pretty
spelling
still
willing
zipper

Circle the correct spelling.

1. misst   missed   mised   missd

2. baloon   balon   ballon   balloon

3. pretty   pertty   preddy   prety

4. ledder   eter   leter   letter

5. differunt   different   diferent   diffrent

6. patturn   patern   pattern   pattren

7. carry   cerry   karry   kerry

8. ziper   zippir   zipper   zippre

Word Meaning

Fill in the missing words.

added	balloon	carry	different	pattern
middle	missed	off	Mississippi	letter
pretty	spelling	still	willing	zipper

1. Did you study for the _____ test?

2. We sailed on the _____ River.

3. I bought a shiny red _____ for my little sister.

4. The _____ on her jacket broke.

5. Will you help me _____ this box into the house?

6. Who wrote you that _____?

7. I went to a _____ school last year.

8. Mother cut out the _____ for a new dress she is making.

My Spelling Dictation

Write the sentences. Circle the spelling words.

1. _____

_____

_____

2. _____

_____

Word Study

Divide these words into syllables.

Remember the rules:

- If a word has double consonants in the middle, divide between them.
- If a word has an ending, divide between the base word and the ending.

1. balloon   _bal loon_   7. zipper   _____

2. spelling   _spell ing_   8. willing   _____

3. pretty   _____   9. middle   _____

4. letter   _____   10. carry   _____

5. added   _____   11. missing   _____

6. pattern   _____   12. Mississippi   _____

Fill in the missing double consonants to make spelling words.

1. spe_____ing   5. pa_____ern

2. o_____   6. mi_____ed

3. sti_____   7. di_____erent

4. mi_____le   8. Mi_____i_____i

Spelling List

This Week's Focus:
- Spell verbs that end with **-ing** or **-ed**
- Spell irregular past tense verbs

STEP 1 Read and Spell

1. swimming
2. swam
3. getting
4. coming
5. came
6. having
7. doing
8. ended
9. happened
10. happening
11. started
12. joked
13. received
14. smiled
15. smiling
16. _____ bonus word
17. _____ bonus word

STEP 2 Copy and Spell

STEP 3 Cover and Spell

fold

Visual Memory

Circle the missing letters. Fill in the blanks.

1. swi __mm__ ing	m	(mm)		7. smi_____ed	l	ll
2. ca_____e	m	mm		8. sti_____	l	ll
3. ge_____ing	t	tt		9. swa_____	m	mm
4. star_____ed	t	tt		10. co_____ing	m	mm
5. en_____ed	d	dd		11. jo_____ed	k	kk
6. ha_____ened	p	pp		12. recei_____ed	v	vv

Write the correct spelling of these words.

1. swiming _____
2. geting _____
3. comeng _____
4. haveng _____
5. dooing _____

6. happend _____
7. happining _____
8. joket _____
9. smild _____
10. kame _____

Fill in the missing word. Use the correct ending.

1. Raul _____ piano lessons last week.
   (start)

2. Have you _____ your birthday present yet?
   (receive)

3. Why is she _____?
   (smile)

Building Spelling Skills, Daily Practice • EMC 6593

Word Meaning

Fill in the correct form of the missing words.

1. We _____ in the river yesterday.
   (swam, swimming)

2. They are going _____ today.
   (swam, swimming)

3. What is _____ on that television program?
   (happened, happening)

4. That is the same thing that _____ on the last show.
   (happened, happening)

5. Who is _____ to the band concert?
   (came, coming)

6. Many people _____ to hear us play last year.
   (came, coming)

7. Karen _____ when she opened the front door.
   (smiling, smiled)

8. Why was she _____?
   (smiling, smiled)

My Spelling Dictation

Write the sentences. Circle the spelling words.

1. _____

   _____

   _____

2. _____

   _____

   _____

Word Study

Write the past tense of these words.
Use the spelling list.

1. joke _____

2. swim _____

3. happen _____

4. come _____

5. end _____

6. smile _____

7. receive _____

8. start _____

Add the ending **ing** to each base word.
What did you do to spell the word correctly?

	no change	double final consonant	drop **e**
1. swim**ming**		✔	
2. get_____			
3. receive_____			
4. come_____			
5. have_____			
6. do_____			
7. smile_____			
8. end_____			
9. happen_____			
10. start_____			
11. joke_____			

Spelling List

This Week's Focus:
- Spell words with long vowel sounds
- Add **-ed** to verbs

STEP 1 Read and Spell	STEP 2 Copy and Spell	STEP 3 Cover and Spell

fold

1. way

2. these

3. niece

4. might

5. show

6. float

7. brain

8. mean

9. close

10. tried

11. cube

12. uniform

13. stayed

14. price

15. usually

16. _____
    bonus word

17. _____
    bonus word

Visual Memory

Unscramble the words. Match them to the correct spelling.

1. yaw	close	8. beuc	price
2. thees	niece	9. ripce	float
3. neice	way	10. mitgh	cube
4. hows	these	11. foalt	uniform
5. anme	tried	12. niarb	brain
6. locse	mean	13. formuni	stayed
7. deirt	show	14. edstay	might

Circle the misspelled words.
Write them correctly on the lines.

1. My new band youniform is silver. _____

2. Cloze the door when you go out. _____

3. The boys mite go fishing next Saturday. _____

4. Put an ice kube in that glass. _____

5. Grandpa staid in bed until 8 o'clock. _____

6. The fox tryed to catch a rabbit. _____

7. Can you shoo me how to play this game? _____

8. Did you ever drink a root beer flote? _____

Word Meaning

Complete the crossword puzzle.

Across

1. not kind
4. the cost
5. special clothing
8. to shut
9. this one and this one

Down

2. a girl relative
3. what you think with
6. the opposite of **sink**
7. a six-sided square
10. to remain

| brain | close | cube | float | mean |
| niece | price | stay | these | uniform |

My Spelling Dictation

Write the sentences. Circle the spelling words.

1. _____

_____

_____

2. _____

_____

_____

Word Study

Circle the letters that make the long vowel sound.
Write the long vowel sound you hear on the line.

1. w(a y) __a__

2. these ____

3. niece ____

4. show ____

5. float ____

6. brain ____

7. mean ____

8. close ____

9. tried ____

10. cube ____

11. uniform ____

12. stayed ____

13. price ____

Add **ed** to the words. Write the words in the correct column.

	no change	change **y** to **i**
1. stay	stayed	
2. try		
3. float		
4. show		
5. cry		
6. hurry		
7. plant		
8. worry		
9. play		
10. scurry		

Spelling List

This Week's Focus:
- Spell words with consonant digraphs **ch**, **sh**, **th**, and **wh**
- Identify the number of syllables in a word
- Recognize the /**sh**/ sound in **sure**

STEP 1 Read and Spell	STEP 2 Copy and Spell	STEP 3 Cover and Spell

fold

1. children
2. search
3. teacher
4. reached
5. think
6. together
7. with
8. where
9. everywhere
10. short
11. push
12. finish
13. sure
14. who
15. whole
16. _____ bonus word
17. _____ bonus word

Visual Memory

Circle all the words that are spelled correctly.

reacht	finush	search
teatcher	whol	where
children	with	chilren
whith	shure	who
think	push	serch
everywere	sure	teacher
whole	poosh	thinck

Circle the misspelled words.
Write them correctly on the lines.

1. Hoo ate that hole cake?

   _____   _____

2. Can the childrun poosh the wagon?

   _____   _____

3. We can go when you finnish the shurt story.

   _____   _____

4. Where do you tink we should serch for it?

   _____   _____

5. Will you and your teecher go there togepher?

   _____   _____

Word Meaning

Answer the questions.

children	search	teacher	reached	think
together	with	where	short	push
everywhere	finish	sure	who	whole

1. Which ones are names for people?

   _____ _____

2. Which word means "all places"?   _____

3. What do you do when you use your brain?   _____

4. Which word means "to complete something"?   _____

5. Which word means "to look for something
   that is lost"?   _____

6. What is the opposite of...?

   part _____   long _____   apart _____

My Spelling Dictation

Write the sentences. Circle the spelling words.

1. _____

   _____

   _____

2. _____

   _____

   _____

Word Study

Fill in the missing letters to make spelling words.
Write **ch**, **th**, **wh**, or **sh**.

1. __ch__ildren

2. sear_____

3. _____ink

4. _____ole

5. _____ere

6. fini_____

7. toge_____er

8. pu_____

9. tea_____er

10. wi_____

11. _____ort

12. _____o

Read the words.
Circle the number of syllables you hear.

1. together   1 2 3 4

2. who   1 2 3 4

3. search   1 2 3 4

4. teacher   1 2 3 4

5. reached   1 2 3 4

6. think   1 2 3 4

7. with   1 2 3 4

8. everywhere   1 2 3 4

9. sure   1 2 3 4

10. children   1 2 3 4

11. whole   1 2 3 4

12. finish   1 2 3 4

13. push   1 2 3 4

14. where   1 2 3 4

15. short   1 2 3 4

Spelling List

This Week's Focus:
• Spell compound words
• Divide compound words into syllables

STEP 1 Read and Spell	**STEP 2** Copy and Spell	**STEP 3** Cover and Spell

fold

1. into

2. today

3. without

4. something

5. become

6. upon

7. myself

8. everybody

9. everyone

10. maybe

11. outside

12. basketball

13. homework

14. skateboard

15. earthquake

16. _____
      bonus word

17. _____
      bonus word

Visual Memory

Find the words hiding in this puzzle.

```
e  v  e  r  y  b  o  d  y  e  s  s
v  a  n  h  o  m  e  w  o  r  k  o
e  r  r  t  o  d  a  y  m  a  a  m
r  w  i  t  h  o  u  t  y  b  t  e
y  o  u  i  h  e  r  o  s  e  e  t
o  u  t  n  o  q  u  d  e  c  b  h
n  e  w  t  t  u  u  y  l  o  o  i
e  u  p  o  n  t  o  a  f  m  a  n
m  a  y  b  e  m  y  s  k  e  r  g
o  u  t  o  u  t  s  i  d  e  d  o
b  a  s  k  e  t  b  a  l  l  i  n
```

become
basketball
earthquake
everybody
everyone
homework
into
maybe
myself
outside
skateboard
something
today
upon
without

Circle the 10 misspelled words.
Write them correctly on the lines.

     Yesterday I finished my homewerk by misef. Then I went owtside and rode my skatbord to the park. Everbody was playing baskutball.

     Evrywon was having fun when sumthing happened. The ground started to shake. It was an erthquak! When it stopped, we ran home wifout the basketball. Maybe it is still at the park.

_____   _____

_____   _____

_____   _____

_____   _____

Word Meaning

Fill in the missing words.

become	basketball	upon	into	everyone
homework	skateboard	maybe	myself	outside
something	earthquake	today	without	everybody

1. Maurice received a _____ for his birthday.

2. An _____ made cracks in the walls of our house.

3. Our teacher said, "There is no _____ _____!"

4. _____ strange ran _____ the barn.

5. Once _____ a time, there was a dragon that couldn't fly.

6. Do you want to _____ a professional soccer player someday?

7. Can you wash the car _____ any help?

8. _____ is gone, so I am all by _____.

My Spelling Dictation

Write the sentences. Circle the spelling words.

1. _____

   _____

   _____

2. _____

   _____

   _____

Use the words in the word box to make compound words.

with	up	to	thing	quake
board	ball	day	every	body
come	side	my	may	home

1. basket _ball_ _____

2. be _____

3. earth _____

4. every _____

5. _____ one

6. _____ work

7. in _____

8. _____ self

9. _____ be

10. out _____

11. skate _____

12. some _____

13. to _____

14. _____ on

15. _____ out

Divide these words into syllables.

1. in|to

2. today

3. without

4. become

5. something

6. maybe

7. outside

8. homework

9. earthquake

Did you discover a new rule here about dividing words into syllables?   Yes   No

What is it? _____

Spelling List

This Week's Focus:
- Spell words with the vowel sound in **small**, **straw**, **song**, and **bought**
- Spell words with the short **u** sound spelled **ough**
- Add the endings **-er** and **-est**

STEP 1 Read and Spell

STEP 2 Copy and Spell

STEP 3 Cover and Spell

fold

1. awful
2. called
3. falling
4. mall
5. small
6. straw
7. drawing
8. strongest
9. longer
10. song
11. along
12. bought
13. brought
14. rough
15. tough
16. _____ bonus word
17. _____ bonus word

Visual Memory

Unscramble the words. Write them on the lines.

falling	awful	called	mall	straw
small	drawing	strongest	longer	tough
song	along	bought	brought	rough

1. awflu _____

2. decall _____

3. llam _____

4. gons _____

5. malls _____

6. olang _____

7. rouhg _____

8. lnoger _____

9. traws _____

10. darwing _____

11. srongtest _____

12. flaling _____

Circle the misspelled words. Write them correctly on the lines.

1. Adam made an ahful mistake.

_____

2. Put the smal starw in the cold drink.

_____ _____

3. He made a drawn of the stronust man in the world.

_____ _____

4. Anna bawght it at the moll.

_____ _____

5. Will you sing a longar sogn next time?

_____ _____

Word Meaning

Answer the questions.

falling	awful	called	mall	straw
small	drawing	strongest	longer	tough
song	along	bought	brought	rough

1. Which word means "terrible"? _____

2. What could be used to make a bed for a farm animal? _____

3. What do you call a place with many shops all together? _____

4. Which word is a kind of picture? _____

5. What is the opposite of...?

   sold _____   shorter _____

   large _____   weakest _____

6. What does **straw** mean in this sentence? Circle your answer.

   I used a plastic straw to drink my milk.

   a. dried hay   b. thin, hollow tube   c. material for making popcorn

My Spelling Dictation

Write the sentences. Circle the spelling words.

1. _____

   _____

   _____

2. _____

   _____

   _____

Word Study

Underline the words with the sound of **a** in **all**.
Circle the letters that make the sound.

(aw)ful	called	tough
mall	song	along
rough	bought	straw
strongest	falling	brought
small	drawing	longer

Add **er** or **est** to make a comparison.

	er	**est**
1. strong	_____	_____
2. long	_____	_____
3. small	_____	_____
4. rough	_____	_____
5. tough	_____	_____

6. That wrestler is the _____ man I've ever seen.
   (strong)

7. Is a rabbit _____ than a cat?
   (small)

8. Mrs. Martin has the _____ bath towels I've ever felt.
   (rough)

9. Billy thinks he is the _____ kid on our block.
   (tough)

10. The yellow bus is _____ than our truck.
    (long)

Spelling List

This Week's Focus:
- Spell words with the long **e** and long **i** sounds spelled **y**
- Spell the plural forms of words by adding **s**, **es**, or **ies**
- Spell the past tense of words by changing **y** to **i** and adding **ed**

STEP 1 Read and Spell

STEP 2 Copy and Spell

STEP 3 Cover and Spell

fold

1. lady
2. ladies
3. surprise
4. surprises
5. toys
6. shoes
7. shy
8. cry
9. cried
10. study
11. studied
12. story
13. only
14. finally
15. family
16. _____
   bonus word
17. _____
   bonus word

Visual Memory

Fill in the missing syllable to make spelling words.

1. la**dy**_____

2. _____ily

3. on_____

4. _____prises

5. _____dies

6. stud_____

7. fi_____ly

8. _____y

9. _____ied

10. sur_____

Circle the misspelled words.
Write them correctly on the lines.

1. The children gave Mother a big suprise.   _____

2. Put on your shoos before you go outside.   _____

3. The baby cryed for his bottle.   _____

4. Do you have a big famuly?   _____

5. Two ladys sang a song.   _____

6. Did you enjoy the storie?   _____

7. The game was finelly over.   _____

8. Have you studyed for the math test?   _____

Word Meaning

Fill in the missing words.

1. What _____ was in that large box?
   (surprise, surprises)

2. Both _____ bought new hats.
   (lady, ladies)

3. Did he _____ clean his bedroom?
   (finally, family)

4. She wants to _____ the violin.
   (study, studied)

5. My grandfather is full of funny _____ that make me laugh.
   (surprise, surprises)

6. I _____ for a long time when my best friend moved away.
   (cry, cried)

My Spelling Dictation

Write the sentences. Circle the spelling words.

1. _____

_____

_____

2. _____

_____

_____

Word Study

Write the words in the correct boxes.

| cry | only | story | my | study | fly |
| lady | why | family | funny | shy | try |

y says **i**	**y** says **e**
cry	

Write the plural forms. Mark how you changed each word.

	add **s**	drop **e**, add **es**	change **y** to **i** and add **es**
1. lady ladies			✔
2. toy _____			
3. story _____			
4. shoe _____			
5. family _____			
6. rocket _____			
7. niece _____			

Spelling List

This Week's Focus:
- Spell words with the vowel sounds in **push** and **do**

STEP 1 Read and Spell	STEP 2 Copy and Spell	STEP 3 Cover and Spell

fold

1. looked
2. good
3. brook
4. football
5. cookie
6. stood
7. full
8. put
9. food
10. school
11. truth
12. room
13. true
14. chew
15. due
16. _____ bonus word
17. _____ bonus word

Visual Memory

Find the words hiding in the puzzle.

```
f  g  t  r  u  t  h  c  h  f
l  o  o  k  e  d  r  o  c  u
f  o  o  d  o  o  k  o  o  l
t  d  p  t  c  h  e  w  o  l
r  u  u  u  b  r  o  o  k  m
u  e  s  p  t  a  t  h  i  h
e  s  c  h  o  o  l  x  e  e
n  o  s  t  o  o  d  l  m  w
```

brook	looked
chew	put
cookie	room
due	school
food	stood
football	true
full	truth
good	

Circle the misspelled words.
Write them correctly on the lines.

1. luked	6. fud	11. truth
2. good	7. full	12. doo
3. brook	8. poot	13. chu
4. futbal	9. stood	14. true
5. cookee	10. schol	15. ruum

_____   _____   _____

_____   _____   _____

_____   _____   _____

Word Meaning

Complete the crossword puzzle.

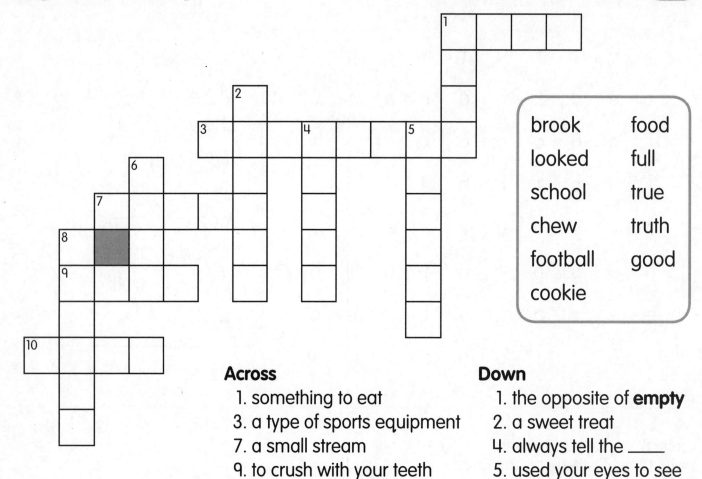

brook   food
looked   full
school   true
chew   truth
football good
cookie

Across

1. something to eat
3. a type of sports equipment
7. a small stream
9. to crush with your teeth
10. the opposite of **bad**

Down

1. the opposite of **empty**
2. a sweet treat
4. always tell the ____
5. used your eyes to see
6. not a lie
8. where you go to learn

My Spelling Dictation

Write the sentences. Circle the spelling words.

1. _____

_____

_____

2. _____

_____

_____

Word Study

Write the words in the correct boxes.

looked	good	truth	put	stood
food	brook	room	true	full
football	school	cookie	chew	due

sound of **u** in **push**	sound of **o** in **do**
looked	

Use the spelling list to find words that are the opposite.

1. empty _____

2. awful _____

3. sat _____

4. remove _____

5. lie _____

6. false _____

Spelling List

This Week's Focus:
- Spell words with **oy** and **oi**
- Spell words with the initial digraph **ch**
- Add the endings **-s**, **-es**, **-ed**, and **-ing**

STEP 1 Read and Spell

STEP 2 Copy and Spell

STEP 3 Cover and Spell

1. pointing
2. oily
3. boy
4. voice
5. oyster
6. voyage
7. loyal
8. joined
9. coin
10. choice
11. poison
12. destroy
13. enjoy
14. choose
15. chocolate
16. _____ bonus word
17. _____ bonus word

Unscramble the words. Match them to the correct spelling.

1. yoil   voice

2. cevoi   oily

3. soyter   boy

4. joyen   voyage

5. yob   oyster

6. agevoy   loyal

7. loyla   enjoy

8. ocin   coin

9. ingpoint   joined

10. cocholate   choice

11. edjoin   chocolate

12. oichce   pointing

13. sonpoi   destroy

14. troydes   poison

Circle the misspelled words. Write them correctly on the lines.

1. My choyse is chocklate.

   _____   _____

2. Did you injoy your voyege?

   _____   _____

3. He will distroy the weeds without using poisen.

   _____   _____

4. The little doy is pointing at an oister.

   _____   _____

5. Which coyn did he chose?

   _____   _____

Word Meaning

Fill in the missing words.

1. We ate _____ on our sea _____.
   (coins, oysters)   (poison, voyage)

2. _____ cake is always Paul's _____.
   (Oyster, Chocolate)   (choose, choice)

3. Did that _____ _____ his toy truck?
   (joined, boy)   (destroy, loyal)

4. Why are you _____ at that gold _____?
   (pointing, oily)   (joined, coin)

5. Don't use a loud _____ while the baby is taking a nap.
   (choice, voice)

6. Lock the box of insect _____ in a cupboard.
   (chocolate, poison)

My Spelling Dictation

Write the sentences. Circle the spelling words.

1. _____

   _____

   _____

2. _____

   _____

   _____

Word Study

Fill in the missing sounds. Write **oi** or **oy**.

1. b_____   4. _____ster   7. p_____son   10. c_____n

2. _____ly   5. v_____ce   8. p_____nting   11. enj_____

3. ch_____ce   6. l_____al   9. destr_____   12. j_____ned

Add endings to change the verbs.

s or es	ed	ing
1. point ___points___	_____	_____
2. join _____	_____	_____
3. smile _____	_____	_____
4. finish _____	_____	_____

Add the correct endings to the verbs.

1. Norman was _____ at the funny television show.
   (smile)

2. The short hand on a clock always _____ to the hour.
   (point)

3. Betty always _____ her work before she plays.
   (finish)

4. Carlos is _____ the Boy Scouts.
   (join)

Spelling List

This Week's Focus:
- Spell contractions
- Recognize homophones **it's** and **its**

STEP 1 Read and Spell	STEP 2 Copy and Spell	STEP 3 Cover and Spell

fold

1. don't
2. didn't
3. I'll
4. I'm
5. it's
6. let's
7. you're
8. we're
9. doesn't
10. o'clock
11. won't
12. wouldn't
13. its
14. can't
15. that's
16. _____ bonus word
17. _____ bonus word

Visual Memory

A contraction is a word formed from two words by leaving out some letters. An apostrophe is used to replace the letters.

Write the apostrophe in the correct place in these contractions.

1. don't
2. didnt
3. Ill
4. thats
5. its

6. cant
7. lets
8. youre
9. were
10. doesnt

11. oclock
12. wont
13. Im
14. wouldnt

Circle the misspelled words.
Write them correctly on the lines.

1. They din't like the scary movie. _____

2. Did you know were moving when school is out? _____

3. Why duzn't the clock work? _____

4. Your going to Disneyland next week! _____

5. Tat's Cindy's pet hamster. _____

6. Its too hot to play outside today. _____

7. Let's ask why they kan't come over. _____

8. A'll bring my football to the game. _____

     Building Spelling Skills, Daily Practice • EMC 6593

Word Meaning

Write the contractions to complete the crossword puzzle.
Don't forget to include the apostrophe.

Down
1. cannot
2. I will
3. does not
5. do not
6. of the clock
7. it is
8. we are

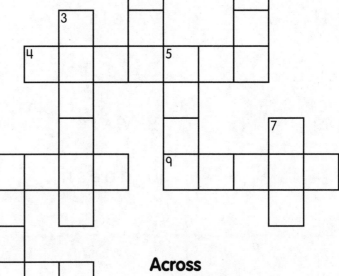

Across
4. would not
8. will not
9. that is
10. you are
11. let us

My Spelling Dictation

Write the sentences. Circle the spelling words.

1. _____

    _____

    _____

2. _____

    _____

    _____

Word Study

Answer the questions.

1. What is the long form of these words?

   won't _____   don't _____

2. Which spelling means "belonging to it"?   its   it's

3. Which spelling means "I will"?   Ill   I'll

What letter or letters are removed to make the contraction?

	contractions	missing letters
1. do not	don't	o
2. we are	_____	_____
3. they are	_____	_____
4. it is	_____	_____
5. would not	_____	_____
6. cannot	_____	_____
7. I am	_____	_____
8. that is	_____	_____
9. does not	_____	_____
10. did not	_____	_____
11. I will	_____	_____
12. let us	_____	_____

Spelling List

This Week's Focus:
• Spell words with the vowel digraphs **ow** and **ou**

STEP 1 Read and Spell	STEP 2 Copy and Spell	STEP 3 Cover and Spell

fold

1. follow

2. below

3. own

4. grown

5. town

6. ground

7. around

8. found

9. about

10. house

11. group

12. would

13. should

14. country

15. cousin

16. _____
   bonus word

17. _____
   bonus word

Visual Memory

Fill in the missing letters. Write **ou** or **ow**.

1. t_____n

2. h_____se

3. gr_____p

4. f_____nd

5. foll_____

6. c_____sin

7. ab_____t

8. _____n

9. bel_____

10. w_____ld

11. ar_____nd

12. gr_____n

13. c_____ntry

14. sh_____ld

15. gr_____nd

Circle the 9 misspelled words in the paragraph.
Write them correctly on the lines.

My kussin went on a hike with a grup of children from toun.

They fallowed a path bello a small hill. They walked arownd

a grove of trees and saw a herd of cows resting on the groun.

Then it was time for everyone to go to my cuzin's howse for lunch.

_____   _____   _____

_____   _____   _____

_____   _____   _____

Word Meaning

Fill in the missing words.

1. The prairie dog _____ is under the _____.
   (below, town)   (country, ground)

2. My _____ lives in a _____ across the ocean.
   (cousin, group)   (country, around)

3. A large _____ of visitors stayed at our _____.
   (own, group)   (house, cousin)

4. The farmer's corn crop _____ be _____ by now.
   (around, should)   (own, grown)

5. Kelly looked all _____ trying to find her lost shoe.
   (around, ground)

6. Do you have your _____ computer at home?
   (town, own)

My Spelling Dictation

Write the sentences. Circle the spelling words.

1. _____

_____

_____

2. _____

_____

_____

Word Study

Listen for the vowel sounds.
Write the words in the correct boxes.

grown	group	ground	about	below
town	follow	would	own	should
found	country	around	cousin	house

sound of **o** in **go**	sound of **ow** in **cow**	sound of **oo** in **too**	sound of **u** in **up**	sound of **u** in **put**

Use words from the spelling list to make rhyming words.

1. shout   _____

2. mouse   _____

3. dozen   _____

4. soup   _____

5. could   _____   _____

6. show   _____   _____

7. ground   _____   _____

8. bone   _____   _____

71

Spelling List

This Week's Focus:
- Review words with long vowel sounds
- Identify long vowels in open syllables

STEP 1 Read and Spell	STEP 2 Copy and Spell	STEP 3 Cover and Spell

(fold)

1. April

2. babies

3. over

4. hello

5. even

6. we

7. silent

8. tiny

9. menu

10. future

11. dear

12. raise

13. white

14. used

15. those

16. _____
   bonus word

17. _____
   bonus word

Visual Memory

Match the parts to make words.
Write the words correctly on the lines.

1. A   ver   1. _April_
2. e   pril   2. _____
3. ba   ny   3. _____
4. si   u   4. _____
5. o   bies   5. _____
6. ti   ven   6. _____
7. men   lent   7. _____
8. fu   ture   8. _____

Circle the misspelled words.
Write the words correctly on the lines.

1. My grandmother says all babys are deer.

   _____   _____

2. Mr. Martin is going to raize tiney roses in his garden.

   _____   _____

3. It was sylent in the cave until someone yelled, "Heloo!"

   _____   _____

4. Last Aprul we painted our fence whyte.

   _____   _____

5. The teacher yousd thoze books in her class.

   _____   _____

Word Meaning

Answer the questions.

April	babies	over	hello	even
we	silent	tiny	menu	future
dear	raise	white	used	those

1. What do you use to choose a meal at a restaurant? _____

2. Which word means...?

    time that hasn't happened yet _____

    above something _____

    not new _____

    a greeting _____

    no sound _____

3. How do you change the word **baby** to make it mean "more than one baby"? _____

4. What month comes after March? _____

My Spelling Dictation

Write the sentences. Circle the spelling words.

1. _____

_____

_____

2. _____

_____

_____

Word Study

Read the words. Listen for a long vowel sound.
Write the words in the correct boxes.

April	raised	used	over	babies
tiny	menu	those	silent	hello
we	white	future	even	

long **a**	long **o**	long **e**	long **i**	long **u**

An open syllable has a vowel at the end. The vowel is usually long.

Divide these words into syllables.
Circle the open syllable in each word.

1. April _____(A)_____ __pril__

2. babies _____ _____

3. over _____ _____

4. hello _____ _____

5. even _____ _____

6. lady _____ _____

7. silent _____ _____

8. tiny _____ _____

9. menu _____ _____

10. future _____ _____

Bonus: vacation _____ _____ _____

       Building Spelling Skills, Daily Practice • EMC 6593

Spelling List

This Week's Focus:
- Spell words with the short **u** sound
- Spell words with the schwa sound
- Review words with long vowel sounds

STEP 1 Read and Spell

STEP 2 Copy and Spell

STEP 3 Cover and Spell

fold

1. disagree
2. again
3. given
4. other
5. money
6. problem
7. does
8. of
9. some
10. laid
11. change
12. tired
13. read
14. nice
15. lower
16. _____
    bonus word
17. _____
    bonus word

Find the words hiding in this puzzle.

a	g	a	i	n	c	h	a	n	g	e	p
l	a	i	d	p	r	o	n	i	o	x	r
o	o	s	v	o	u	t	t	c	c	f	o
w	m	o	n	e	y	h	r	e	a	d	b
e	e	m	g	q	n	e	b	y	n	o	l
r	h	e	e	t	i	r	e	d	t	e	e
a	g	d	i	s	a	g	r	e	e	s	m

again	nice
change	of
disagree	other
does	problem
given	read
laid	some
lower	tired
money	

Circle the 12 misspelled words.
Write them correctly on the lines.

Jack had a prblum yesterday. He wanted to red a good

book, so he went to a nyce bookstore. Jack picke out a book and

handed his muney to the clerk.

Jack said to the clerk, "This is not the write chanje."

The clerk counted the monny agin. Jack was rite. The clerk

gave him some more mony, and Jack went home to reed his book.

_____   _____   _____

_____   _____   _____

_____   _____   _____

_____

Word Meaning

Fill in the missing words.

again	change	disagree	does	given
laid	lower	money	nice	of
other	problem	read	some	tired

1. _____ Arthur have enough _____ to buy a ticket?

2. Did the _____ lady help you solve your _____?

3. I _____ with what I just _____ in the newspaper.

4. My hen _____ some _____ her eggs in the weeds behind the chicken coop.

5. Harry was _____ five dollars for cutting Mrs. Murphy's lawn.

6. Would you like to have _____ of my chocolate bar?

My Spelling Dictation

Write the sentences. Circle the spelling words.

1. _____

_____

_____

2. _____

_____

_____

Word Study

Underline the words that have the schwa sound.
Circle the letters that make the sound.

a̶bout   lesso̶n

1. disagree	6. tired	11. problem
2. again	7. given	12. used
3. lower	8. nice	13. silent
4. laid	9. read	14. those
5. change	10. raise	15. tiny

Fill in the blank with a rhyming spelling word.

other	money	read	laid
change	nice	tired	some

1. arrange _____   5. bread _____

2. fired _____   6. twice _____

3. honey _____   7. brother _____

4. paid _____   8. drum _____

STEP 1 — Read and Spell

fold

1. city
2. cereal
3. face
4. could
5. guess
6. huge
7. age
8. danger
9. goose
10. gone
11. coast
12. clean
13. guard
14. giant
15. carton
16. _____ bonus word
17. _____ bonus word

STEP 2 — Copy and Spell

STEP 3 — Cover and Spell

Visual Memory

Find the words hiding in this puzzle.

```
c  e  r  e  a  l  a  g  e  d  o
g  i  g  u  a  r  d  o  m  a  c
u  o  t  c  a  r  t  o  n  n  o
e  x  n  y  c  e  r  s  h  g  u
s  s  e  e  f  a  c  e  u  e  l
s  a  n  g  i  a  n  t  g  r  d
c  o  a  s  t  q  c  l  e  a  n
```

age	face
carton	giant
cereal	gone
city	goose
clean	guard
coast	guess
could	huge
danger	

Circle the misspelled words.
Write them correctly on the lines.

1. age
2. cartun
3. sereal
4. citee
5. clean

6. koast
7. could
8. danjer
9. fase
10. giant

11. gawn
12. goose
13. gard
14. guess
15. huje

_____   _____   _____

_____   _____   _____

_____   _____   _____

                   Building Spelling Skills, Daily Practice • EMC 6593

Fill in the missing words.

coast	city	age	guess
danger	clean	guard	giant

1. The movie star had a _____ to protect her.

2. Have you ever been to New York _____?

3. The warning sign read "_____! Falling rocks."

4. The magician could _____ a person's _____.

5. Did you help _____ up the beach on Saturday?

6. Why does she always buy _____-sized packages of everything?

7. I can see sailboats off the _____.

My Spelling Dictation

Write the sentences. Circle the spelling words.

1. _____

_____

_____

2. _____

_____

_____

Word Study

The letters **c** and **g** make a hard and a soft sound.

Read each word and listen to the sound of the bolded letter.
Write it in the correct box.

age	**g**iant	**c**lean	**c**oast	fa**c**e
carton	**g**one	**g**uess	**c**ould	**g**oose
cereal	**c**ity	hu**g**e	dan**g**er	**g**uard

c		g	
hard /**k**/	soft /**s**/	hard /**g**/	soft /**j**/

Fill in the blanks with spelling words that mean the opposite.

1. country _____   3. safety _____

2. tiny _____   4. dirty _____

Fill in the missing spelling words and their opposites.

1. When faced with _____, he ran for _____.

2. The _____ goat hid from the _____ wolf.

3. He was _____ in class this morning, but is _____ now.

This Week's Focus:
• Spell r-controlled words with **or**, **er**, **ir**, **ur**, and **ear**

STEP 1 Read and Spell	STEP 2 Copy and Spell	STEP 3 Cover and Spell
1. word		
2. work		
3. world		
4. were		
5. first		
6. girl		
7. turned		
8. learn		
9. bird		
10. fire		
11. here		
12. nurse		
13. jury		
14. stirred		
15. wear		
16. _____ bonus word		
17. _____ bonus word		

fold

Visual Memory

Unscramble the words. Write them on the lines.

word	were	turned	fire	jury
work	first	learn	here	stirred
world	girl	bird	nurse	wear

1. rowk _____

2. drow _____

3. gril _____

4. laern _____

5. fier _____

6. weer _____

7. nuser _____

8. brid _____

9. rowld _____

10. yurj _____

11. frist _____

12. raew _____

13. ternud _____

14. sterrid _____

15. reeh _____

Circle the 9 misspelled words.
Write them correctly on the lines.

Raul was on his way to wurk when he tirned a corner and saw a house on frie. Ferst, he called 911. Then, he looked around the house.

Raul herd a gril calling for help. He helped her crawl out a window.

At the hospital, a nurse took good care of the gerl. The child said, "I want to lurn how to be a nurs when I grow up."

_____   _____   _____

_____   _____   _____

_____   _____   _____

Word Meaning

Answer the questions.

word	work	world	were	first
girl	turned	learn	bird	fire
here	nurse	jury	stirred	wear

1. Who helps sick and injured people? _____

2. Which spelling word means...? the earth _____

   flames _____

   mixed it up _____

3. What do you call letters put together to represent something? _____

4. Who decides if a person is innocent or guilty of a crime? _____

5. Which spelling word is the opposite of ...?

   last _____   boy _____

   play _____   there _____

My Spelling Dictation

Write the sentences. Circle the spelling words.

1. _____

   _____

   _____

2. _____

   _____

   _____

Word Study

Circle the letters that make the /er/ sound in these words.

1. first   3. turned   5. word   7. faster

2. learn   4. girl   6. were   8. work

Fill in the missing letters to make spelling words. Write **er**, **ir**, **ur**, **ear**, or **or**.

1. n_____se   3. w_____e   5. l_____n   7. w_____d

2. b_____d   4. w_____ld   6. quick_____   8. st_____red

Write the spelling word that rhymes with each of these words.

word	work	world	were	first
girl	learn	fire	wear	nurse

1. care _____   4. burst _____   7. bird _____

2. fur _____   5. curl _____   8. liar _____

3. clerk _____   6. fern _____   9. purse _____

Fill in the missing spelling words.

1. What are you going to _____ to the party?

2. Where _____ the boys going in such a hurry?

3. My dad has to _____ in the garden this Saturday.

4. Her mother is a _____ in Dr. Chan's office.

Spelling List

This Week's Focus:
• Spell r-controlled words with **ar**, **are**, **or**, and **ore**

STEP 1 Read and Spell

fold

1. aren't
2. partner
3. hard
4. chart
5. farm
6. start
7. large
8. more
9. before
10. horse
11. north
12. morning
13. care
14. stare
15. warning
16. _____ bonus word
17. _____ bonus word

STEP 2 Copy and Spell

STEP 3 Cover and Spell

Visual Memory

Match the parts to make a spelling word.
Write the complete word on the line.

1. far	th	1.	farm
2. lar	n't	2.	_____
3. nor	m	3.	_____
4. are	re	4.	_____
5. sta	ge	5.	_____
6. warn	fore	6.	_____
7. be	ner	7.	_____
8. part	ing	8.	_____

Circle the misspelled words.
Write them correctly on the lines.

1. arent	6. narth	11. hourse
2. care	7. stayr	12. partnur
3. mor	8. morning	13. hard
4. charte	9. befor	14. warning
5. farm	10. start	15. larje

_____   _____   _____

_____   _____   _____

Word Meaning

Fill in the missing words.

1. His _____ rode off _____ daybreak.
   (partner, start)   (horse, before)

2. Is it hard work to run a _____ _____?
   (care, large)   (more, farm)

3. We must _____ on our trip early in the _____.
   (start, warning)   (before, morning)

4. Read the _____ on the _____ before you dive in.
   (morning, warning)   (start, chart)

5. It isn't polite to _____ at people.
   (care, stare)

6. The explorer had a _____ trip going by dog sled.
   (north, hard)

My Spelling Dictation

Write the sentences. Circle the spelling words.

1. _____

   _____

   _____

2. _____

   _____

   _____

Word Study

Fill in the missing letters to make a spelling word.
Write **ar**, **or**, **are**, or **ore**.

1. p__ar__tner

2. n_____th

3. m_____ning

4. c_____

5. h_____d

6. _____en't

7. bef_____

8. w_____ning

9. st_____

10. l_____ge

11. m_____e

12. ch_____t

13. st_____t

14. h_____se

15. f_____m

Write the opposite of each word from your spelling list.

1. easy _____

2. tiny _____

3. less _____

4. after _____

5. south _____

6. evening _____

7. finish _____

Fill in the missing spelling words and their opposites.

1. The _____ giant and the _____ elf were friends.

2. I take a walk in the _____ and again in the _____.

3. Migrating birds fly _____ in the fall and _____ in the spring.

4. I do my homework _____ dinner, and then I play _____ dinner.

Spelling List

This Week's Focus:
- Spell words with the vowel sounds in **to**, **top**, **wall**, and **up**
- Recognize homophones **threw** and **through**
- Spell words with suffixes **-less** and **-ful**

STEP 1 Read and Spell

STEP 2 Copy and Spell

STEP 3 Cover and Spell

fold

1. threw
2. through
3. thoughtless
4. caught
5. fault
6. taught
7. because
8. one
9. once
10. water
11. watch
12. wanted
13. wonder
14. wonderful
15. walk
16. _____
   bonus word
17. _____
   bonus word

Find the words hiding in this puzzle.

```
w  a  n  t  e  d  e  d  b  e  c
t  h  o  u  g  h  t  l  e  s  s
h  r  t  a  u  g  h  t  c  w  o
r  e  w  a  t  e  r  o  a  o  n
e  w  a  a  n  d  o  o  u  n  c
w  f  a  u  l  t  u  n  s  d  e
w  a  t  c  h  k  g  w  e  e  t
o  n  c  a  u  g  h  t  x  r  e
n  w  o  n  d  e  r  f  u  l  d
```

because	through
caught	walk
fault	wanted
once	watch
one	water
taught	wonder
thoughtless	wonderful
threw	

Circle the misspelled words.
Write them correctly on the lines.

1. wundir
2. caught
3. walk
4. wunce
5. becuz

6. tawght
7. thoughtless
8. watur
9. through
10. fawlt

11. wanted
12. throo
13. wach
14. onederful
15. one

_____   _____   _____

_____   _____   _____

_____   _____   _____

Word Meaning

Answer the questions.

threw	walk	one	through	wonderful
once	water	wonder	watch	thoughtless
caught	wanted	because	fault	taught

1. Which spelling words rhyme with ...?

   bought _____ _____

   new _____ _____

2. What does **watch** mean in this sentence? Circle your answer.
   You must watch your step when you climb a ladder.

   a. be careful   b. something that tells time   c. standing guard

3. Which word means "only one time"? _____

4. What is the past tense of ...?

   catch _____   teach _____

   throw _____   want _____

My Spelling Dictation

Write the sentences. Circle the spelling words.

1. _____

   _____

   _____

2. _____

   _____

   _____

Word Study

Read the words. Listen for the vowel sounds.
Write each word in the correct box.

wanted	water	through	walk
threw	because	watch	taught
thought	caught	fault	

sound of **a** in **wall**	sound of **oo** in **too**

Add the correct suffix to the words.

-less means "without"   **-ful** means "filled with"

1. Morris had a _____ surprise.
   (wonder)

2. It was _____ of you to be late for the party.
   (thought)

3. The _____ man helped fix the flat tire.
   (thought)

4. I always feel _____ on my birthday.
   (joy)

5. A newborn kitten is _____.
   (help)

6. Will you be _____ and clean up that mess?
   (help)

Spelling List

This Week's Focus:
- Spell words that end with **or**, **ar**, and **er**
- Spell words with the final long **e** sound spelled **y**

STEP 1 Read and Spell

STEP 2 Copy and Spell

STEP 3 Cover and Spell

fold

1. color
2. odor
3. farmer
4. calendar
5. dollar
6. party
7. liar
8. after
9. number
10. better
11. doctor
12. weather
13. every
14. forty
15. sugar
16. _____
   bonus word
17. _____
   bonus word

Visual Memory

Match the parts. Write the words on the lines.

1. co	y	1. _color_
2. calen	ber	2. _____
3. part	lor	3. _____
4. ev	dar	4. _____
5. num	ery	5. _____
6. o	gar	6. _____
7. doc	dor	7. _____
8. for	tor	8. _____
9. su	ty	9. _____
10. weath	ter	10. _____
11. bet	er	11. _____

Circle the misspelled words. Write them correctly on the lines.

1. The calender cost one doller.

   _____ _____

2. Dad had a big partie when he turned fourty.

   _____ _____

3. You had bettir see the doctur about that bad cold.

   _____ _____

4. What nummer comes after nine?

   _____

5. Evry flower in the garden has a sweet oder.

   _____ _____

Word Meaning

Answer these questions.

color	odor	farmer	dollar	calendar
party	liar	after	number	better
doctor	weather	every	sugar	forty

1. Which letters make the /**er**/ sound in these words?

   liar _____   after _____   odor _____

2. What do you call someone who helps sick people?   _____

3. What do you call someone who is not truthful?   _____

4. Which spelling word has the /**sh**/ sound in **she**?   _____

5. Which spelling word means "all"?   _____

6. What is the opposite of...?

   before _____   worse _____

My Spelling Dictation

Write the sentences. Circle the spelling words.

1. _____

   _____

   _____

2. _____

   _____

   _____

Word Study

Underline all the words that have the /er/ sound in **her**.
Circle the letters that make the /er/ sound.

col(or)   every   better

odor   calendar   sugar

party   watch   dollar

march   number   liar

weather   after   farmer

Divide the words into syllables.

1. color   col or

2. calendar _____

3. better _____

4. dollar _____

5. farmer _____

6. number _____

7. party _____

8. liar _____

9. weather _____

10. odor _____

11. after _____

12. sugar _____

Building Spelling Skills

WEEK 25

Spelling List

This Week's Focus:
- Spell words with the /f/ sound spelled **ph**, **gh**, and **f**
- Spell words with the base word **happy**
- Spell words with the suffixes **-ly** and **-ness**

STEP 1 Read and Spell

STEP 2 Copy and Spell

STEP 3 Cover and Spell

fold

1. phone
2. photograph
3. orphan
4. alphabet
5. graph
6. nephew
7. enough
8. father
9. half
10. Friday
11. cough
12. unhappy
13. happier
14. happily
15. happiness
16. _____ bonus word
17. _____ bonus word

Visual Memory

Match the parts to make a spelling word.
Write the complete word on the line.

1. Fri	phan		1. _____
2. fa	ew		2. _____
3. or	day		3. _____
4. neph	nough		4. _____
5. e	ther		5. _____
6. pho	hap	py	6. _____
7. al	to	bet	7. _____
8. un	pha	graph	8. _____

Circle the misspelled words.
Write them correctly on the lines.

1. fone	5. fotograph	9. orfan
2. haf	6. fadder	10. happiness
3. alfabet	7. nefew	11. enuf
4. cough	8. graph	12. Fritay

_____   _____   _____

_____   _____   _____

_____   _____   _____

Word Meaning

Answer the questions.

phone	orphan	nephew	happiness	cough
alphabet	graph	enough	Friday	photograph
father	half	unhappy	happier	happily

1. What do you call a picture taken with a camera? _____

2. What is the word for a child with no parents? _____

3. What is a name for all the letters from **a** to **z**? _____

4. Which spelling word means "all that is needed"? _____

5. What do you do when you have a bad cold? _____

6. Which spelling words are names for family members?

_____ _____

My Spelling Dictation

Write the sentences. Circle the spelling words.

1. _____

_____

_____

2. _____

_____

_____

Word Study

Sometimes the digraph **ph** and **gh** stand for the /f/ sound.
Fill in the missing letters. Write **f**, **ph**, or **gh**.

1. _ph_one

2. enou____

3. or____an

4. ____ather

5. ____riday

6. ne____ew

7. hal____

8. gra____

9. al____abet

10. ____otogra____

Fill in the missing letters to complete the spelling word.

1. Grandmother has an old ph_____ of her mother.

2. The first-grade teacher wrote the _____ph_____ on the chalkboard.

3. I ate _____f of the chicken on F_____.

A suffix is something you add to the end of words to change the meaning.
Change these words by adding a suffix.

ly means "in this way"   **ness** means "the state of being"

1. She climbed _____ and _____ up the ladder.
   (slow)   (careful)

2. The explorers were surrounded by _____ inside the cave.
   (dark)

3. Red Riding Hood skipped along _____ to Grandma's house.
   (happy)

4. His _____ filled my heart with _____.
   (kind)   (happy)

Spelling List

This Week's Focus:
- Spell words with silent letters
- Spell words with the prefixes **un-** and **re-**

STEP 1 Read and Spell	**STEP 2** Copy and Spell	**STEP 3** Cover and Spell

fold

1. ghost
2. neighbor
3. high
4. knew
5. knot
6. unknown
7. rewrap
8. wrong
9. written
10. wrapper
11. unwrap
12. climb
13. limb
14. gnaw
15. gnat
16. _____ bonus word
17. _____ bonus word

Visual Memory

Find the words hiding in this puzzle.

```
g  h  o  s  t  k  n  e  w  z
n  e  i  g  h  b  o  r  r  w
k  x  g  g  i  r  l  e  i  r
n  w  n  n  h  k  i  w  t  a
o  r  o  a  a  g  m  r  t  p
t  o  t  t  s  w  b  a  e  p
u  n  k  n  o  w  n  p  n  e
o  g  u  m  c  l  i  m  b  r
i  n  u  n  w  r  a  p  g  o
```

climb	neighbor
ghost	rewrap
gnat	unknown
gnaw	unwrap
high	wrapper
knew	written
knot	wrong
limb	

Circle the misspelled words.
Write them correctly on the lines.

1. gost
2. naybor
3. hi
4. gnat

5. knot
6. knoo
7. unknone
8. rewrap

9. rong
10. written
11. onwrap
12. clim

13. limb
14. naw

_____ _____ _____

_____ _____ _____

_____ _____ _____

15. The ribbon was tied in a not. _____

16. Little nats flew around the fruit tree. _____

17. A lim broke off the tree during the storm. _____

Word Meaning

Complete the crossword puzzle.

Across

1. not known
4. to move up a ladder
6. to take off the covering
8. the spirit of someone dead
   seen by a person
9. a fastening made by tying
   string together

Down

2. a person who lives next door
3. the opposite of **right**
5. words were put on paper
7. a small insect
8. to chew on

ghost	high	gnaw	limb	knot
written	knew	unknown	unwrap	wrong
rewrap	climb	gnat	neighbor	

My Spelling Dictation

Write the sentences. Circle the spelling words.

1. _____

   _____

   _____

2. _____

   _____

   _____

Word Study

Read each word.
Mark an X over the silent letters.

Ẍrap   Ẍnot

ghost   limb   knot   unwrap

high   knew   rewrap   climb

gnaw   write   wrong   gnat

Write the correct prefix in front of each word.

un means "not"
unhappy means "not happy"

re means "again"
reread means "read again"

1. My cat tore the paper on the gift, so Mother had to _____ it.
   (wrap)

2. The name of the artist was _____.
   (known)

3. People were _____ of what to do after the earthquake.
   (sure)

4. My homework paper was messy, so I had to _____ it.
   (write)

5. _____ the present to see what is inside.
   (Wrap)

6. Uncle Ted must _____ the fence every five years.
   (paint)

Spelling List

This Week's Focus:
- Spell words with the suffixes -**ful**, -**ly**, -**less**, -**er**, and -**est**

STEP 1 Read and Spell

STEP 2 Copy and Spell

STEP 3 Cover and Spell

fold

1. useful
2. quietly
3. slowly
4. careful
5. careless
6. quickly
7. useless
8. worthless
9. fearful
10. fearless
11. joyful
12. smarter
13. fastest
14. funniest
15. happiest
16. _____ bonus word
17. _____ bonus word

Visual Memory

Write the missing suffix to make a spelling word.

> ful   ly   less   er

1. use _ful____   5. smart_____   9. care_____

2. use_____   6. slow_____   10. care_____

3. quiet_____   7. joy_____   11. fear_____

4. worth_____   8. fast_____   12. fear_____

Circle the misspelled words.
Write them correctly on the lines.

1. Mother walked slooly and kwietly past the sleeping baby.

   _____   _____

2. Carla was joyfull when she won the ribbon for fastist runner in school.

   _____   _____

3. It is useles to do the job if you are kareless.

   _____   _____

4. Pete is the happyest person I know.

   _____

5. A feerless shepherd quikly chased away the hungry wolf.

   _____   _____

Word Meaning

Answer the questions.

useful	quietly	slowly	careful	quickly
careless	useless	fearful	joyful	worthless
smarter	fastest	fearless	funniest	happiest

1. What do these words do?   **smarter**   **fastest**

   a. name something   b. compare something   c. describe something

2. What do these words do?   **thoughtless**   **useful**

   a. name something   b. compare something   c. describe something

3. Which spelling word is the opposite of ...?

   quickly _____   useful _____

   careless _____   saddest _____

4. Which word means "afraid"?   _____

My Spelling Dictation

Write the sentences. Circle the spelling words.

1. _____

   _____

   _____

2. _____

   _____

   _____

Word Study

Add the suffix **est** to these words.
Mark what you did to change the word.

	no change	double final consonant	change **y** to **i**
1. fast _fastest_	✔		
2. happy _____			
3. quick _____			
4. funny _____			
5. sad _____			
6. big _____			
7. smart _____			
8. silly _____			
9. small _____			

Add suffixes to the words to complete the sentences. Write **ful** or **less**.

1. Be care_____ as you work so you don't make a care_____ mistake.

2. The fear_____ firefighter rescued the fear_____ boy from the tree.

3. One sock is use_____, but two socks are use_____.

Building Spelling Skills

Spelling List

This Week's Focus:
- Spell words with the long **a**, long **e**, and short **e** sounds
- Spell words in the **-other**, **-ead**, **-eat**, and **-ear** word families
- Recognize the /**ur**/ sound in **heard** and **early**

STEP 1 Read and Spell

STEP 2 Copy and Spell

STEP 3 Cover and Spell

fold

1. brother
2. mother
3. another
4. field
5. friend
6. heard
7. early
8. friendly
9. head
10. near
11. year
12. shield
13. eat
14. measure
15. break
16. _____ bonus word
17. _____ bonus word

Visual Memory

Find the words hiding in this puzzle.

```
m  e  a  s  u  r  e  e  a  a
o  n  e  h  e  a  r  d  n  n
t  r  y  i  e  l  f  s  o  b
h  x  n  e  n  d  i  e  t  r
e  e  e  l  a  h  e  a  h  e
r  a  a  d  o  r  l  r  e  a
n  t  r  d  e  a  d  l  r  k
f  r  i  e  n  d  l  y  o  r
a  n  o  b  r  o  t  h  e  r
```

another	head
break	heard
brother	measure
early	mother
eat	near
field	shield
friendly	year

Circle the misspelled words. Write them correctly on the lines.

1. My muther and bruther have the same birthday.

   _____ _____

2. Trina hurd from an old frend today.

   _____ _____

3. We herd a noise in the empty feeld next door.

   _____ _____

4. Erly next yeer they are moving to Texas.

   _____ _____

5. May I eta unother slice of pie?

   _____ _____

Word Meaning

Complete the crossword puzzle.

Across

1. close by
3. the opposite of **sister**
7. a female parent
10. a piece of armor
12. listened to
13. a person who knows and likes another person

Down

2. the opposite of **late**
4. to chew and swallow food
5. to find the size of something
6. the top part of your body
8. to smash
9. an open area with few trees
11. January 1 to December 31

break	brother	friend	field	near
head	heard	measure	year	
shield	mother	eat	early	

My Spelling Dictation

Write the sentences. Circle the spelling words.

1. _____

   _____

   _____

2. _____

   _____

   _____

Word Study

Read the words. Listen for the vowel sounds.
Write the words in the correct boxes.

eat	friend	break	measure
head	field	shield	

long **e**	long **a**	short **e**

Change the beginning sounds to create new words.

_____mother	_____ead	_____eat	_____ear
_____other	_____ead	_____eat	_____ear
_____other	_____ead	_____eat	_____ear
_____other	_____ead	_____eat	_____ear

Spelling List

This Week's Focus:
- Recognize homophones
- Review words with long vowel sounds

STEP 1 Read and Spell

fold

1. they're
2. there
3. their
4. soup
5. night
6. knight
7. right
8. write
9. weight
10. wait
11. piece
12. peace
13. hour
14. our
15. wrote
16. _____
   bonus word
17. _____
   bonus word

STEP 2 Copy and Spell

STEP 3 Cover and Spell

Visual Memory

Match the scrambled word to the correct spelling.

1. ecape	their	7. twai	right
2. ousp	soup	8. peice	wait
3. threi	there	9. rou	piece
4. heret	peace	10. hrou	wrote
5. ightn	write	11. ritgh	hour
6. ritwe	night	12. rwote	our

Circle the misspelled words. Write them correctly on the lines.

1. Their going to get they're books.

   _____   _____

2. The brave night saved a princess last nite.

   _____   _____

3. Mom said to weight here for an howr.

   _____   _____

4. Hour friends came to dinner last nitgh.

   _____   _____

5. May I have a peace of there pizza?

   _____   _____

6. Can you right a recipe for that soop?

   _____   _____

Word Meaning

Fill in the missing words.

1. Can you put _____ coats in the closet over _____?
   (their, there)   (they're, there)

2. The _____'s fight lasted all _____ long.
   (knight, night)   (knight, night)

3. Try to _____ the spelling word _____ this time.
   (right, write)   (right, write)

4. We spent an _____ with _____ grandfather.
   (our, hour)   (our, hour)

5. What is the _____ of that huge hog?
   (wait, weight)

6. That _____ of paper is a _____ treaty.
   (peace, piece)   (peace, piece)

My Spelling Dictation

Write the sentences. Circle the spelling words.

1. _____

   _____

   _____

2. _____

   _____

   _____

Word Study

Read the words. Listen for the vowel sounds.
Write the words in the correct boxes.
Circle the letters that spell the sounds.

wait	peace	night	right	piece	stare
write	weight	beach	stair	sight	plane
flee	knight	plain	beech	flea	site

long **a**	long **i**	long **e**
w(a i)t		

Write the opposite of each word from the spelling list.

1. erase _____   4. left _____

2. day _____   5. war _____

3. here _____   6. whole _____

Fill in the missing words.

1. If you _____ the word wrong, make it _____.

2. The generals signed the _____ treaty late one _____.

Building Spelling Skills

WEEK 30

Spelling List

This Week's Focus:
- Review long and short vowel sounds
- Review how to divide words into syllables

STEP 1 Read and Spell

STEP 2 Copy and Spell

STEP 3 Cover and Spell

fold

1. air
2. against
3. all right
4. until
5. presents
6. beautiful
7. favorite
8. clothes
9. people
10. vacation
11. remember
12. already
13. hospital
14. minute
15. straight
16. _____ bonus word
17. _____ bonus word

Visual Memory

Match the parts to make spelling words.
Write the complete words on the lines.

1. a	ents		1. _____
2. un	ute		2. _____
3. pres	gainst		3. _____
4. peo	til		4. _____
5. min	ple		5. _____
6. beau	ca	ber	6. _____
7. va	read	ful	7. _____
8. re	ti	tal	8. _____
9. al	pi	y	9. _____
10. hos	mem	tion	10. _____

Circle the misspelled words.
Write them correctly on the lines.

1. air	6. bootiful	11. already
2. alright	7. favrute	12. remimber
3. strate	8. clothes	13. hospital
4. against	9. peeple	14. minite
5. presunts	10. vacashun	15. until

_____   _____   _____

_____   _____   _____

_____   _____   _____

Word Meaning

Complete the crossword puzzle.

Down

1. a place for the care of the sick or injured
2. not crooked
3. very pretty
5. men, women, and children
6. the one you like best

Across

4. gifts
7. a time of rest from school or work
8. what people wear
9. happened before this time
10. don't forget

| already | clothes | people | remember | hospital |
| beautiful | favorite | presents | straight | vacation |

My Spelling Dictation

Write the sentences. Circle the spelling words.

1. _____

   _____

   _____

2. _____

   _____

   _____

Word Study

Circle the letters in the words that make the given sound.

short **u**	until
short **i**	minute until
long **i**	all right
long **o**	clothes
long **e**	already remember
long **a**	favorite straight vacation

Divide the words into syllables.

1. against _a   gainst_   6. vacation _____

2. presents _____   7. minute _____

3. beautiful _____   8. hospital _____

4. favorite _____   9. already _____

5. people _____   10. remember _____

© Evan-Moor Corp.   123   Building Spelling Skills, Daily Practice • EMC 6593

My Spelling Tests

Using Your Spelling Test Forms:

First

Use the following pages for your Friday spelling tests. Write your answers on these forms.

Then

Record your score on your spelling record form on pages 156 and 157.

Spelling Test

Listen to the words.
Write each word on a line.

_____
date

1. _____

2. _____

3. _____

4. _____

5. _____

6. _____

7. _____

8. _____

9. _____

10. _____

11. _____

12. _____

13. _____

14. _____

15. _____

16. _____

17. _____

Listen to the sentences.
Write them on the lines.

1. _____

_____

_____

2. _____

_____

_____

Spelling Test

Listen to the words.
Write each word on a line.

_____
date

1. _____

2. _____

3. _____

4. _____

5. _____

6. _____

7. _____

8. _____

9. _____

10. _____

11. _____

12. _____

13. _____

14. _____

15. _____

16. _____

17. _____

Listen to the sentences.
Write them on the lines.

1. _____

_____

_____

2. _____

_____

_____

Spelling Test

Listen to the words.
Write each word on a line.

_____
date

1. _____

2. _____

3. _____

4. _____

5. _____

6. _____

7. _____

8. _____

9. _____

10. _____

11. _____

12. _____

13. _____

14. _____

15. _____

16. _____

17. _____

Listen to the sentences.
Write them on the lines.

1. _____

_____

_____

_____

2. _____

_____

_____

_____

Spelling Test

Listen to the words.
Write each word on a line.

_____
date

1. _____

2. _____

3. _____

4. _____

5. _____

6. _____

7. _____

8. _____

9. _____

10. _____

11. _____

12. _____

13. _____

14. _____

15. _____

16. _____

17. _____

Listen to the sentences.
Write them on the lines.

1. _____

_____

_____

2. _____

_____

_____

Spelling Test

Listen to the words.
Write each word on a line.

_____
date

1. _____

2. _____

3. _____

4. _____

5. _____

6. _____

7. _____

8. _____

9. _____

10. _____

11. _____

12. _____

13. _____

14. _____

15. _____

16. _____

17. _____

Listen to the sentences.
Write them on the lines.

1. _____

_____

_____

2. _____

_____

_____

Spelling Test

Listen to the words.
Write each word on a line.

_____
date

1. _____

2. _____

3. _____

4. _____

5. _____

6. _____

7. _____

8. _____

9. _____

10. _____

11. _____

12. _____

13. _____

14. _____

15. _____

16. _____

17. _____

Listen to the sentences.
Write them on the lines.

1. _____

_____

_____

2. _____

_____

_____

Spelling Test

Listen to the words.
Write each word on a line.

_____
date

1. _____

2. _____

3. _____

4. _____

5. _____

6. _____

7. _____

8. _____

9. _____

10. _____

11. _____

12. _____

13. _____

14. _____

15. _____

16. _____

17. _____

Listen to the sentences.
Write them on the lines.

1. _____

_____

_____

2. _____

_____

_____

Spelling Test

Listen to the words.
Write each word on a line.

_____
date

1. _____

2. _____

3. _____

4. _____

5. _____

6. _____

7. _____

8. _____

9. _____

10. _____

11. _____

12. _____

13. _____

14. _____

15. _____

16. _____

17. _____

Listen to the sentences.
Write them on the lines.

1. _____

_____

_____

2. _____

_____

_____

Spelling Test

Listen to the words.
Write each word on a line.

date

1. _____

2. _____

3. _____

4. _____

5. _____

6. _____

7. _____

8. _____

9. _____

10. _____

11. _____

12. _____

13. _____

14. _____

15. _____

16. _____

17. _____

Listen to the sentences.
Write them on the lines.

1. _____

_____

_____

2. _____

_____

_____

Spelling Test

Listen to the words.
Write each word on a line.

_____
date

1. _____

2. _____

3. _____

4. _____

5. _____

6. _____

7. _____

8. _____

9. _____

10. _____

11. _____

12. _____

13. _____

14. _____

15. _____

16. _____

17. _____

Listen to the sentences.
Write them on the lines.

1. _____

_____

_____

2. _____

_____

_____

Spelling Test

Listen to the words.
Write each word on a line.

_____
date

1. _____

2. _____

3. _____

4. _____

5. _____

6. _____

7. _____

8. _____

9. _____

10. _____

11. _____

12. _____

13. _____

14. _____

15. _____

16. _____

17. _____

Listen to the sentences.
Write them on the lines.

1. _____

_____

_____

2. _____

_____

_____

Spelling Test

Listen to the words.
Write each word on a line.

_____
date

1. _____

2. _____

3. _____

4. _____

5. _____

6. _____

7. _____

8. _____

9. _____

10. _____

11. _____

12. _____

13. _____

14. _____

15. _____

16. _____

17. _____

Listen to the sentences.
Write them on the lines.

1. _____

_____

_____

2. _____

_____

_____

Spelling Test

Listen to the words.
Write each word on a line.

_____
date

1. _____

2. _____

3. _____

4. _____

5. _____

6. _____

7. _____

8. _____

9. _____

10. _____

11. _____

12. _____

13. _____

14. _____

15. _____

16. _____

17. _____

Listen to the sentences.
Write them on the lines.

1. _____

_____

_____

2. _____

_____

_____

Spelling Test

Listen to the words.
Write each word on a line.

_____
date

1. _____

2. _____

3. _____

4. _____

5. _____

6. _____

7. _____

8. _____

9. _____

10. _____

11. _____

12. _____

13. _____

14. _____

15. _____

16. _____

17. _____

Listen to the sentences.
Write them on the lines.

1. _____

_____

_____

2. _____

_____

_____

Spelling Test

Listen to the words.
Write each word on a line.

_____
date

1. _____

2. _____

3. _____

4. _____

5. _____

6. _____

7. _____

8. _____

9. _____

10. _____

11. _____

12. _____

13. _____

14. _____

15. _____

16. _____

17. _____

Listen to the sentences.
Write them on the lines.

1. _____

_____

_____

2. _____

_____

_____

Spelling Test

Listen to the words.
Write each word on a line.

_____
date

1. _____

2. _____

3. _____

4. _____

5. _____

6. _____

7. _____

8. _____

9. _____

10. _____

11. _____

12. _____

13. _____

14. _____

15. _____

16. _____

17. _____

Listen to the sentences.
Write them on the lines.

1. _____

_____

_____

2. _____

_____

_____

Spelling Test

Listen to the words.
Write each word on a line.

_____
date

1. _____

2. _____

3. _____

4. _____

5. _____

6. _____

7. _____

8. _____

9. _____

10. _____

11. _____

12. _____

13. _____

14. _____

15. _____

16. _____

17. _____

Listen to the sentences.
Write them on the lines.

1. _____

   _____

   _____

2. _____

   _____

   _____

Spelling Test

Listen to the words.
Write each word on a line.

_____
date

1. _____

2. _____

3. _____

4. _____

5. _____

6. _____

7. _____

8. _____

9. _____

10. _____

11. _____

12. _____

13. _____

14. _____

15. _____

16. _____

17. _____

Listen to the sentences.
Write them on the lines.

1. _____

_____

_____

2. _____

_____

_____

Spelling Test

Listen to the words.
Write each word on a line.

_____
date

1. _____

2. _____

3. _____

4. _____

5. _____

6. _____

7. _____

8. _____

9. _____

10. _____

11. _____

12. _____

13. _____

14. _____

15. _____

16. _____

17. _____

Listen to the sentences.
Write them on the lines.

1. _____

_____

_____

2. _____

_____

_____

Spelling Test

Listen to the words.
Write each word on a line.

_____
date

1. _____

2. _____

3. _____

4. _____

5. _____

6. _____

7. _____

8. _____

9. _____

10. _____

11. _____

12. _____

13. _____

14. _____

15. _____

16. _____

17. _____

Listen to the sentences.
Write them on the lines.

1. _____

_____

_____

2. _____

_____

_____

Spelling Test

Listen to the words.
Write each word on a line.

_____
date

1. _____

2. _____

3. _____

4. _____

5. _____

6. _____

7. _____

8. _____

9. _____

10. _____

11. _____

12. _____

13. _____

14. _____

15. _____

16. _____

17. _____

Listen to the sentences.
Write them on the lines.

1. _____

_____

_____

2. _____

_____

_____

Spelling Test

Listen to the words.
Write each word on a line.

_____
date

1. _____

2. _____

3. _____

4. _____

5. _____

6. _____

7. _____

8. _____

9. _____

10. _____

11. _____

12. _____

13. _____

14. _____

15. _____

16. _____

17. _____

Listen to the sentences.
Write them on the lines.

1. _____

_____

_____

2. _____

_____

_____

Spelling Test

Listen to the words.
Write each word on a line.

_____
date

1. _____

2. _____

3. _____

4. _____

5. _____

6. _____

7. _____

8. _____

9. _____

10. _____

11. _____

12. _____

13. _____

14. _____

15. _____

16. _____

17. _____

Listen to the sentences.
Write them on the lines.

1. _____

   _____

   _____

2. _____

   _____

   _____

Spelling Test

Listen to the words.
Write each word on a line.

_____
date

1. _____

2. _____

3. _____

4. _____

5. _____

6. _____

7. _____

8. _____

9. _____

10. _____

11. _____

12. _____

13. _____

14. _____

15. _____

16. _____

17. _____

Listen to the sentences.
Write them on the lines.

1. _____

_____

_____

2. _____

_____

_____

Spelling Test

Listen to the words.
Write each word on a line.

_____
date

1. _____

2. _____

3. _____

4. _____

5. _____

6. _____

7. _____

8. _____

9. _____

10. _____

11. _____

12. _____

13. _____

14. _____

15. _____

16. _____

17. _____

Listen to the sentences.
Write them on the lines.

1. _____

_____

_____

2. _____

_____

_____

Spelling Test

Listen to the words.
Write each word on a line.

_____
date

1. _____

2. _____

3. _____

4. _____

5. _____

6. _____

7. _____

8. _____

9. _____

10. _____

11. _____

12. _____

13. _____

14. _____

15. _____

16. _____

17. _____

Listen to the sentences.
Write them on the lines.

1. _____

_____

_____

2. _____

_____

_____

Spelling Test

Listen to the words.
Write each word on a line.

_____
date

1. _____

2. _____

3. _____

4. _____

5. _____

6. _____

7. _____

8. _____

9. _____

10. _____

11. _____

12. _____

13. _____

14. _____

15. _____

16. _____

17. _____

Listen to the sentences.
Write them on the lines.

1. _____

_____

_____

2. _____

_____

_____

Spelling Test

Listen to the words.
Write each word on a line.

_____
date

1. _____

2. _____

3. _____

4. _____

5. _____

6. _____

7. _____

8. _____

9. _____

10. _____

11. _____

12. _____

13. _____

14. _____

15. _____

16. _____

17. _____

Listen to the sentences.
Write them on the lines.

1. _____

_____

_____

2. _____

_____

Spelling Test

Listen to the words.
Write each word on a line.

_____
date

1. _____

2. _____

3. _____

4. _____

5. _____

6. _____

7. _____

8. _____

9. _____

10. _____

11. _____

12. _____

13. _____

14. _____

15. _____

16. _____

17. _____

Listen to the sentences.
Write them on the lines.

1. _____

_____

_____

2. _____

_____

_____

Spelling Test

Listen to the words.
Write each word on a line.

_____
date

1. _____

2. _____

3. _____

4. _____

5. _____

6. _____

7. _____

8. _____

9. _____

10. _____

11. _____

12. _____

13. _____

14. _____

15. _____

16. _____

17. _____

Listen to the sentences.
Write them on the lines.

1. _____

_____

_____

2. _____

_____

_____

My Spelling Record

Week	Date	Number Correct	Words Missed
1			
2			
3			
4			
5			
6			
7			
8			
9			
10			
11			
12			
13			
14			
15			

My Spelling Record

Week	Date	Number Correct	Words Missed
16			
17			
18			
19			
20			
21			
22			
23			
24			
25			
26			
27			
28			
29			
30			